LET'S FIND OUT! **THE HUMAN BODY**

T0082226

THE SKIN ON YOUR BODY

HEIDI CHANG

Britannica®
Educational Publishing

IN ASSOCIATION WITH

ROSEN
EDUCATIONAL SERVICES

Published in 2015 by Britannica Educational Publishing (a trademark of Encyclopædia Britannica, Inc.) in association with The Rosen Publishing Group, Inc.
29 East 21st Street, New York, NY 10010

Distributed exclusively by Rosen Publishing.
To see additional Britannica Educational Publishing titles, go to rosenpublishing.com.

First Edition

Britannica Educational Publishing
J. E. Luebering: Director, Core Reference Group
Mary Rose McCudden: Editor, Britannica Student Encyclopedia

Rosen Publishing
Hope Lourie Killcoyne: Executive Editor
Tracey Baptiste: Editor
Nelson Sá: Art Director
Nicole Russo: Designer
Cindy Reiman: Photography Manager

Library of Congress Cataloging-in-Publication Data

Chang, Heidi, author.
The skin on your body/Heidi Chang. — First edition.
    pages cm. — (Let's find out! The human body)
Includes bibliographical references and index.
ISBN 978-1-62275-644-5 (library bound) — ISBN 978-1-62275-645-2 (pbk.) —
ISBN 978-1-62275-646-9 (6-pack)
1. Skin — Juvenile literature. 2. Skin — Diseases — Juvenile literature. 3. Human body — Juvenile literature. 4. Human physiology — Juvenile literature. I. Title.
QM484.C43 2015
612.7'9 — dc23
                                                                        2014016777

Manufactured in the United States of America

Photo credits: Cover, interior pages background Fedorov Oleksiy/Shutterstock.com; p. 1 Todd Kuhns/Shutterstock.com; p. 4 Kristina Zhuravleva/Shutterstock.com; p. 5 Dorling Kindersley/Vetta/Getty Images; p. 6 joSon/Iconica/Getty Images; p. 7 milanrajce/iStock/Thinkstock; p. 8 Kuttelvaserova Stuchelova/Shutterstock.com; p. 9 Leonardo Cameiro Photographic Art/Moment/Getty Images; p. 10 Steve Gschmeissner/Science Photo Library/Getty Images; p. 11 LucyLooLoo/Shutterstock.com; p. 12 Bele Olmez/Getty Images; p. 13 leonello calvetti/Shutterstock.com; p. 14 imagebroker.net/SuperStock; p. 15 Cheryl Casey/Shutterstock.com; p. 16 artemisphoto/Shutterstock.com;. p. 17 pixologicstudio/iStock/Thinkstock; p. 18 Inga Marchuk/Shutterstock.com; p. 19 Diego Cervo/Shutterstock.com; p. 20 pedalist/Shutterstock.com; p. 21 Lisa F. Young/Shutterstock.com; p. 22 John Kaprielian/Science Source; p. 23 Fuse/Getty Images; p. 24 Kameel4u/Shutterstock.com; p. 25 3445128471/Shutterstock.com; p. 26 Dmitry Naumov/Shutterstock.com; p. 27 BestPhotoStudio/Shutterstock.com; p. 28 Erika Ray/Moment/Getty Images; p. 29 Comstock/Stockbyte/Thinkstock.

CONTENTS

What Is Skin?

Skin is the outer covering that humans and all other animals with a backbone have. Human skin has three layers. Each layer has a special job. The outer layer is called the epidermis. The epidermis is the layer of skin that we can see. It keeps the inside of the body safe. It helps keep germs out of our bodies.

The second layer, or dermis, makes the epidermis strong. It carries blood to the epidermis. The blood feeds skin cells to keep the skin healthy.

Skin is different on different parts of the body. Some places have thinner or thicker layers of skin.

A cell is the basic unit of life. All living things are made up of cells.

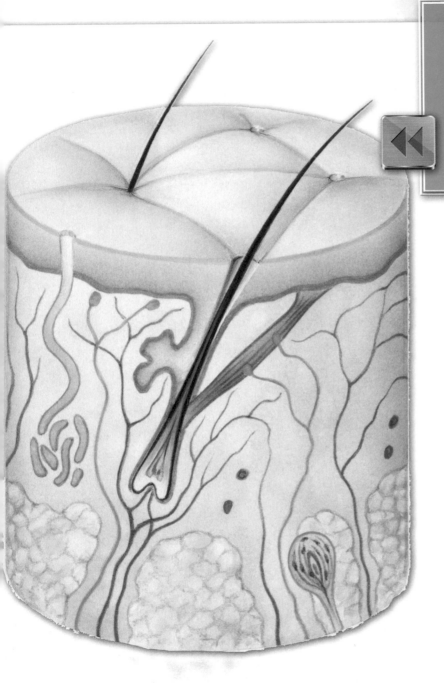

This shows all three layers of the skin, with the pores on the top layer, hair coming out of the second layer, and fat in the third layer.

This layer also has nerves that help us to feel the things in the world around us. The bottom layer is made up of mostly fat. This fat supplies nutrients to the other two layers. The bottom layer connects the skin to all the tissues underneath it. It also cushions the body and protects it from the cold.

Different People, Different Skin

Everybody has skin, but each person's skin looks different. Cells in the skin produce a substance called melanin, which creates different skin colors. Melanin protects our skin from the Sun's harmful rays. The melanin in dark skin is more active than the melanin in light skin. That means that

People may share the same skin color because they come from the same family or their ancestors came from the same part of the world.

people with darker skin have better protection from the Sun.

Skin of all colors can be damaged by the Sun, however. Too much sun can cause sunburns, when the skin becomes red and warm. Very bad sunburns can cause blisters to form.

Some people have no active melanin. This condition is called albinism. Albinos cannot make skin color. Their

THINK ABOUT IT

One form of skin cancer is called melanoma. Where does that name come from?

7

skin is almost white or pink. They must be very careful in sunlight because they have no protection against the Sun's rays.

All skin has the same structure, but it can look very different on the body. The skin on the palms of hands and the bottoms of feet is very thick. Thick skin protects us as we walk and touch things. The skin on eyelids is very thin. That is why you can still see the glow of a bright light even with your eyes closed.

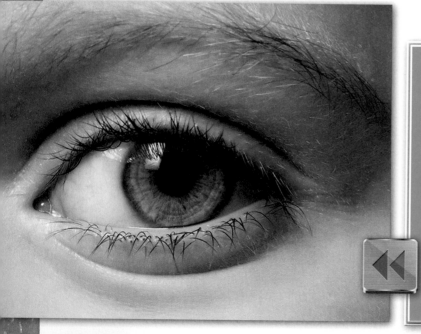

Some babies' eye color changes in their first year of life. This is because babies have less active melanin. After their first birthday, eye color is usually permanent.

No two people have the same fingerprint. Even identical twins have different fingerprints.

Some parts of the skin have a lot of hair, such as the head. Other areas have no hair at all, such as the lips. The skin on the nose and forehead can be very oily. But the chin and jaw area are usually dry.

On our fingertips and the bottoms of our feet, the skin has tiny ridges that make a pattern that is different for everyone.

THINK ABOUT IT

Why is the skin different on different parts of the body?

The Skin Grows and Heals

Have you ever seen a snake shed its skin? Your body does that, too, but not all at once like a snake. Skin never stops growing. Dead cells of the outer layer constantly flake off as new ones form. This also helps the skin to heal.

The skin has many blood vessels. If the skin gets hurt, the blood vessels may break. The skin turns purple or blue in color because blood

This picture is an up-close look at some dead skin cells.

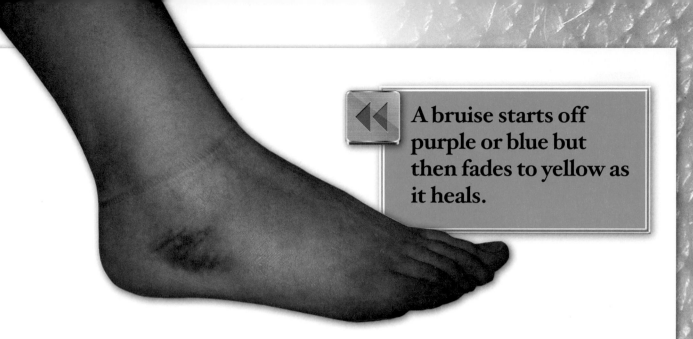

A bruise starts off purple or blue but then fades to yellow as it heals.

cells have leaked out below the skin. This is called a bruise. In lighter skin, a bruise is more easily seen than in darker skin.

When the skin is cut open, blood flows outside of the body. Some of the blood dries as a hard cover over the wound. This is a scab. The scab stays in place until the skin heals.

COMPARE AND CONTRAST

How is a snake's skin different from a human's skin?

Skin Keeps Us Warm

The skin knows when we are cold. When the skin senses cold, tiny muscles in the skin contract. This response makes the hairs on the skin stand up. It gives us little bumps called goose bumps. They trap heat inside the skin like a coat. The fat in the third layer of skin also protects us from the cold.

Goose bumps are formed by a reflex action. That means we cannot control when they happen.

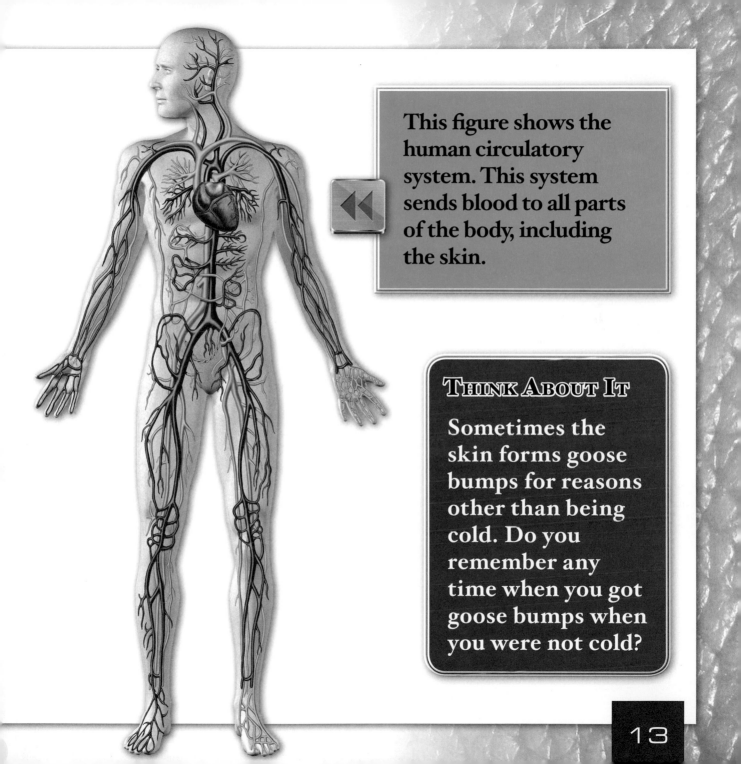

This figure shows the human circulatory system. This system sends blood to all parts of the body, including the skin.

THINK ABOUT IT

Sometimes the skin forms goose bumps for reasons other than being cold. Do you remember any time when you got goose bumps when you were not cold?

THE SKIN GLANDS

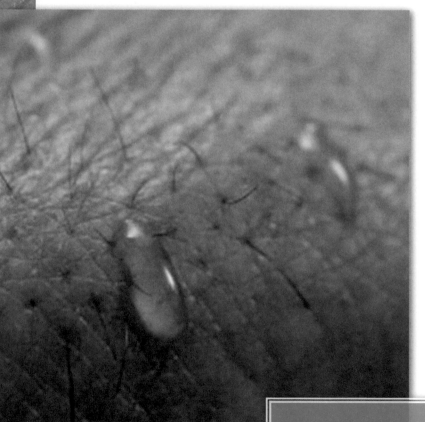

The skin has two kinds of glands: oil glands and sweat glands. Oil glands send oil through our pores to the top layer of skin. Oil helps keep the skin soft and flexible. Sweat glands help cool the body.

 The hands, feet, and armpits have the most sweat glands.

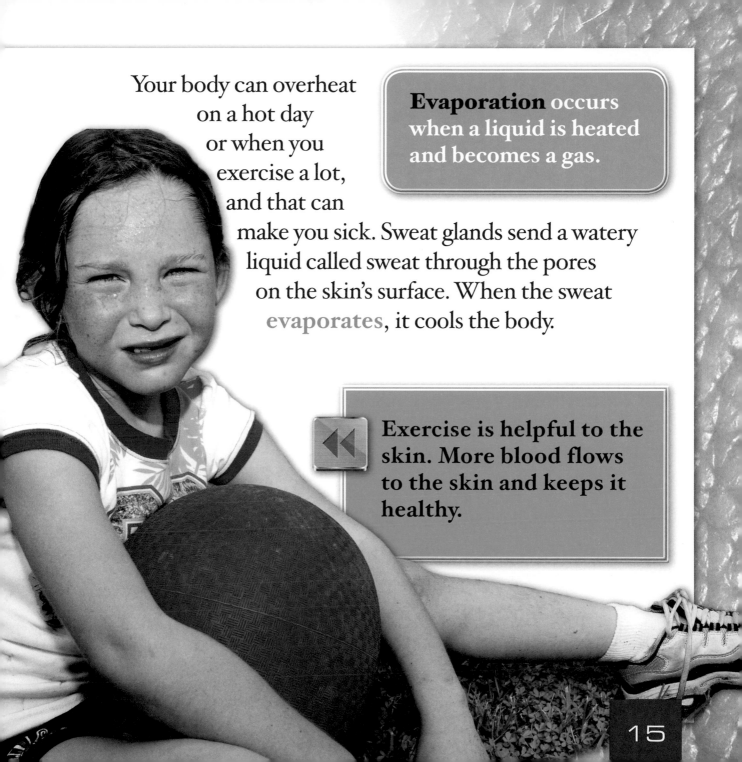

Your body can overheat on a hot day or when you exercise a lot, and that can make you sick. Sweat glands send a watery liquid called sweat through the pores on the skin's surface. When the sweat evaporates, it cools the body.

Evaporation occurs when a liquid is heated and becomes a gas.

Exercise is helpful to the skin. More blood flows to the skin and keeps it healthy.

A Warning Against Danger

How do you know if something is hot or cold? What happens when something falls on your toe? We get to know our world because skin can feel. The skin has many nerve cells. They send messages to the brain. The brain then returns messages

Feet, hands, and lips have more nerves than other parts of the body.

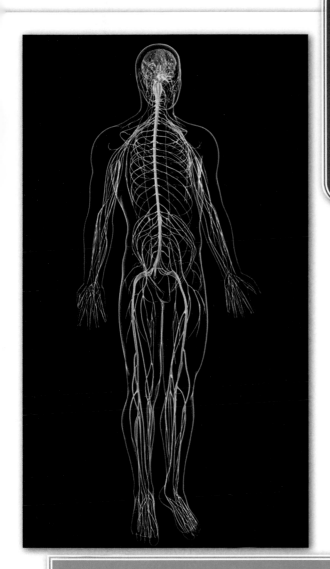

to the body, telling it how to respond. This allows us to sense hot and cold and to feel pain.

Even if we don't see a sharp object or a hot stove, we can feel it. Our body quickly pulls away. This response is called a reflex. It is an action that we do without thinking about it. Without signals from the nerves in our skin, we might get cut or badly burned.

Nerve endings are attached to different types of receptors on the skin. They help us to feel hot and cold, identify pain, and respond to pressure.

How Skin Changes

At birth the skin is soft and flexible. As the body gets older, the skin begins to change. In **adolescence**, the skin is still soft. But the oil glands start to make more oil. This extra oil clumps together with dead skin cells to clog the pores. This makes small bumps called pimples.

A baby's skin heals faster than an adult's skin because it is still growing fast!

As adults, the top layer of skin begins to thin. Then the skin makes fewer cells. The glands make less oil. The top layer becomes dry and less soft. The skin folds over on itself, forming wrinkles. Older skin takes longer to heal.

Weather can change skin, too. Sunlight, wind, and pollution can damage skin. Exposure to the Sun's rays over time can cause skin cancer. Cold weather and strong winds can cause the skin to become dry and chapped.

Adolescence is the time in life between childhood and adulthood.

Wrinkles can also be caused by environmental factors like pollution or by what we eat and drink.

Nails and Hair

Special cells in the skin thicken to form nails and hair. Nails protect the fingers and toes. They can also help us to use or pick up small objects. They help us to scratch. Nails never stop growing.

Both nails and hair are types of skin.

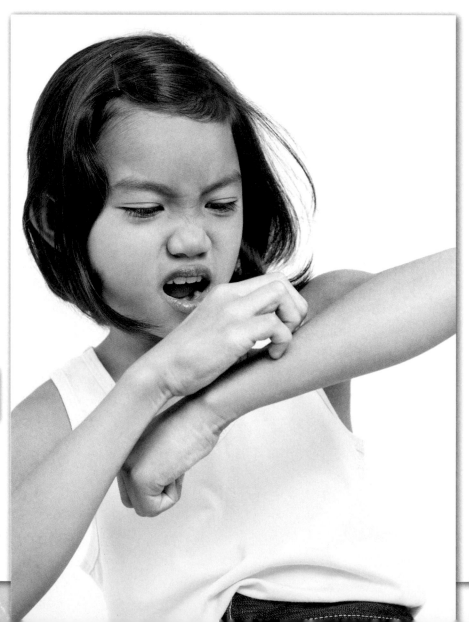

Hair has many jobs. Eyelashes and brows keep dust and dirt out of our eyes. Hair can also provide protection for our heads from the Sun. As people get older, they may begin to lose the hair on their head.

People have different colored hair. This is because of melanin. When hair turns white or gray, it is because the hair has stopped making melanin.

As people age, their hair may turn gray or white and they may begin to lose some of their hair.

COMPARE AND CONTRAST

How are nails, hair, and skin the same?

Skin Problems

Have you ever gotten red bumps on your skin? Those itchy red bumps are the body's way of protecting us. The body is reacting to something it thinks is dangerous. It might be an allergic reaction to something we touched. It might be a bug bite. The skin is busy trying to get rid of whatever it thinks might harm us. Once it is gone, the skin clears up.

The body may take a few days to react to an allergy. Luckily, an allergic reaction can't be passed on to someone else.

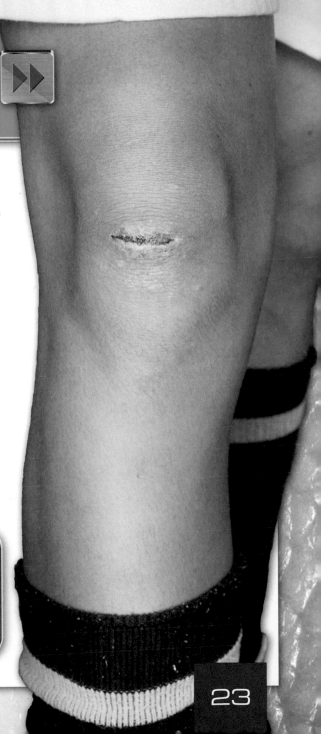

Keeping the skin around a cut clean helps it to heal more quickly.

▶▶

Cuts and bruises also damage our skin. Tiny paper cuts can hurt, but they do not go deep into the skin. The skin quickly makes new cells that fill the cut. Deeper cuts take longer to heal.

Too much oil can cause a condition called acne. Skin burns can be caused by heat, chemicals, or too much exposure to the Sun. Several types of cancer can also start in the skin.

COMPARE AND CONTRAST

How are allergies and bug bites the same?

Skin and the Weather

If skin is exposed to very cold weather, it can become hard, cold, and bloodless. The toes, fingers, ears, and nose may lose feeling. This reaction to **severe** cold is called frostbite. In the event of frostbite, it is important to get the area warm. Warm water works

In cold weather, blood vessels tighten and release so only a little blood gets to the skin. This can make hands and cheeks look red.

Severe means serious.

best. In the worst cases, frostbite may damage the skin so badly that it needs to be cut off.

In very hot weather, sweat may not be enough to cool down the body. If the body gets too hot, the sweat glands can run out of moisture. Then the skin cannot cool us down. This reaction to extreme heat is called heatstroke.

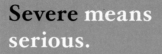

It is important to drink lots of water on very hot days.

How to Protect Your Skin

The skin protects our body, so we need to protect our skin! In cold weather, you should cover your skin. A coat, hat, and mittens trap the heat inside us. Shoes keep our feet from harm.

On a hot day, we need different clothing. The right kind of hat, such

Sunblock must be applied every few hours in order to protect our skin from the Sun's rays.

How can clothing protect the skin in hot weather?

The Sun's rays are strongest between 10 AM and 2 PM. That is when skin needs the most protection.

as one with a visor or broad rim, gives the skin shade from the Sun. Sunblock lotion and bug repellent keep the skin protected. Remember to drink plenty of water! The skin needs water to make sweat so we can cool down!

FUN FACTS ABOUT SKIN

1. The skin is the largest organ in the body.

2. Believe it or not, your skin weighs more than your brain! An adult's skin can weigh about 8 pounds (3.6 kilograms).

3. Skin can show how you are feeling! When we are scared or feel shy, skin can get goose bumps or turn red.

4. What grows faster, your fingernails or toenails? Fingernails! Both grow faster in the summer than in winter.

Skin can shed up to 9 pounds (4 kilograms) of cells in one year!

5. It does not hurt when we cut our hair and nails. Why? They are no longer living cells. They are only alive below the skin.

6. Where on your body is the skin most thin? Your eyelids!

7. Where is the epidermis the thickest? The bottoms of the feet and the palms of the hands!

8. Scars may be a different color than the rest of your skin. They are also tough and do not produce sweat or hair.

Skin helps us to feel and understand the world around us.

GLOSSARY

blood vessels Hollow tubes that carry blood throughout the body.

core The central or most important part.

flexible Able to bend easily and not break.

function What something can do.

germs Tiny living things that can cause disease in a plant or animal.

layer One thickness of something over or under another.

moisture A small amount of liquid.

muscles Tissues that shrink and stretch to help the body move.

plug To fill or close a hole.

pollution The result of dirtying air, land, or water with harmful substances.

protect To keep something from being hurt.

reacting Acting in response to something else.

repellent A substance that helps to keep something away.

replaced Used something in place of another.

response An answer to something.

ridges Raised areas.

scratch To scrape or rub with fingernails or toenails.

shed To lose.

shrink To become small.

signals Messages that give notice to start something.

surface The outside part of something.

tough Very hard or firm.

visor The part of a hat that sticks out in front.

FOR MORE INFORMATION

Books

Baines, Becky. *ZigZag: Your Skin Holds You In: A Book About Your Skin*. Washington, DC: National Geographic Children's Books, 2008.

Caster, Shannon. *Skin*. New York, NY: Rosen Publishing Group, 2010.

Guillain, Charlotte. *Our Skin*. Chicago, IL: Heinemann-Raintree Library, 2010.

Seuling, Barbara. *Your Skin Weighs More Than Your Brain: and Other Freaky Facts About Your Skin, Skeleton, and Other Body Parts*. North Mankato, MN: Capstone Press, 2007.

Silverstein, Alvin, and Virginia Silverstein. *Handy Health Guide to Burns and Blisters*. Berkeley Heights, NJ: Enslow Publishers, 2014.

Websites

Because of the changing nature of Internet links, Rosen Publishing has developed an online list of websites related to the subject of this book. The site is updated regularly. Please use this link to access the list:

http://www.rosenlinks.com/LFO/Skin

INDEX